MINDFULNESS FOR A PEACEFUL EXISTENCE

by

Dr. Margo DelaGarza

Thank you
Jonathan and Cesar

Table of Contents

People want to be happy. Everyone I've ever worked with has said they want to be happy. However, nobody seems to know *how* to be happy. This book was written to help you discover how to live a genuinely peaceful and happy life. Although we can't be happy all the time, we can live in such a way that for the most part, we experience a sense of happiness and contentment.

We will explore questions that are designed to help you see things in a new way. I will explain what mindfulness is and how to practice mindfulness. What I've found though, is that there are some persistent thoughts and beliefs that make it very difficult for some people to maintain a state of mindfulness for more than a few seconds. I will specifically address the most common areas (identity, love, relationships, etc) in which thoughts predominate, in order to create some space for presence to emerge.

The inquiry is an essential part of the process. It's not enough for me to tell you about it. It's important that you experience what is presented, not just think about it or talk about it. It's not something that can be handed over to you. You have to create the experience for yourself.

What is mindfulness?

Mindfulness is giving your full attention to the present moment. All of your attention is focused on this moment, not on the past or future. It means being awake to life, as it is really occurring, and not judging or thinking about it. Just experiencing it. For practical purposes, the word mindfulness is being used to indicate the state of being fully attentive in the present moment. In reality, when you are completely alert in the present moment, your mind is not really "full". The state of being fully alert in the present moment is more accurately described as "mind-lessness", in which the mind is not full of thoughts, but instead the thinking mind is less active, just aware, with less thoughts.

For most people, their mind is almost always thinking. Their attention is hijacked by thoughts about the past (what has already happened), and thoughts about the future (what is going to happen). Most people think they think their own thoughts, but in reality, thinking is happening to them. If you were really in control of your own thoughts, would you ever have unpleasant thoughts? The fact that most human beings constantly think about negative things indicates that they are not actually thinking their own thoughts, but thinking is happening to them.

The goal is to be able to be so focused that you are able to think at will, and that you create some space between you and your thoughts so that when thoughts happen to you, you are able to bring your attention back to the present moment and not spiral downward. You can do this by paying attention to the present moment in order to interrupt the stream of unpleasant thoughts. You can't be thinking about the past or future and be fully present in the moment at the same time. By practicing mindfulness, you will begin to use your mind in a very powerful way instead of being a victim of the incessant negative thoughts that plague you right now.

Mindfulness is about living your life moment by moment, as if it really mattered. Most of the time we're not paying attention to what's happening right now.

- Pay close attention to your breathing, especially when you're feeling intense emotions.
- Notice the sights, sounds, and smells in this moment, bring them to your conscious awareness.
- Recognize that your thoughts and emotions are fleeting and do not define you, an insight that can free you from negative thought patterns.
- Tune into your body's physical sensations, from the water hitting your skin in the shower to the way your body rests in your office chair.

Why is mindfulness so hard?

Mindfulness can seem so hard because it feels like as soon as you become present thinking almost immediately resumes...so it feels like you never stop thinking. Living a truly present life is a skill that you learn, so the key is to keep bringing yourself back to the present moment. Your mind might be so active that it feels like for every 60 seconds you have to bring yourself back 55 times. If that's the case, stay with it. Over time, you will notice that the gaps between thoughts become longer. You will eventually get to a point where you can stop thinking at will. A lot of people get discouraged and say mindfulness doesn't work for them. It only doesn't work if you stop doing it.

Present Moment Reality Check

On a scale from 1 to 10, how at peace and at ease are you right now? If it's not at a 9 or a 10, ask yourself what keeps it from being higher?

Look around the room. What is actually happening? You might be sitting in a chair. You may have comfortable clothes on, sitting in a comfortable room. You probably ate today and have a roof over your head. Probably nobody is kicking you right now and nothing unpleasant is happening to you right now.

Is anything wrong right now? Do you have any problems right now? Your mind might begin to argue that yes, you have lots of problems. If you just focus on your actual experience in the present moment (reality), not on thoughts (non-reality), you'll notice that you don't have any problems right now. If you stay focused on the reality of this present moment, can the number go up at all? Most of the time you should be at a 9 or a 10. There will be times when this is not possible, but this should be very rare, like when you've experienced the loss of someone close to you. Even when challenging situations arise, you can still remain in a state of peace.

Your mind might be arguing that there's no way you can be at a 9 or 10 most of the time. Why do you think this is? Some people become so used to their negative thoughts and unhappiness that they can't even imagine they could be happy. It almost seems 'wrong' to be happy. Some people are actually addicted to their suffering. Seriously consider the *actual* reasons why you can't be at a 9 or 10 right now or most of the time.

How to know if you have unresolved issues

When you do a present moment reality check and you're not at a 10, then ask yourself what keeps you from being at a 10. Your answer may be: I feel anxious, or I feel sad. Ask yourself what you're anxious about, what you're sad about. If you don't know, ask yourself the first time you remember feeling that way. Whatever comes up is the starting point for healing the unresolved issue.

Stay Here

A powerful exercise for practicing present moment awareness is to silently repeat to yourself 'stay here', 'stay here'. Throughout the day, remind yourself to stay here as your thoughts attempt to sweep you away from reality, away from the present moment, away from life itself. Keep reminding yourself to stay here. Commit to being fully alive by staying here, by being attentive to the present moment, the only moment in which you are actually alive.

You are not your thoughts

You are not your thoughts. You have thoughts, but you are not your thoughts. This is a very important point because what makes some thoughts so distressing is that we identify with the thoughts. Being identified with thoughts means that your identity, or sense of self, is attached to the thought. If the thought comes up that "I'm unlovable" and I believe it's true, my actions will reflect the beliefs of someone who is unlovable. Begin dis-identifying with your thoughts by telling yourself "I don't have to believe everything that I think". Take the judgment out of it.

Instead of focusing on right and wrong and on whose fault it is, just ask yourself "does this work for me?" If it doesn't work for you, drop it. This takes courage. You will often find that honoring your truth means not making other people happy or not looking good in the eyes of others.

Your mind might argue with a lot of the information presented in order to keep you in a state of unhappiness. It will trick you into thinking that this is not useful or that it doesn't work for you. Just notice the thoughts and remain alert and present.

"When you run after your thoughts, you are like a dog chasing a stick: every time a stick is thrown, you run after it. Instead, be like a lion who, rather than chasing after the stick, turns to face the thrower. One only throws a stick at a lion once. " ~ Milarepa

Who are you, really?

There is a "you" that exists, that consists of your identity. For the purposes of this conversation, I will propose that there's the 'real' you and there's the 'you' created by thoughts, opinions, life experiences, social conditioning, etc. Let's call that the conceptualized you.

The real you is the you that's been there from the very start, when your little heartbeat started in your mother's womb. There was a life form, and it became 'you'. The real you is the part of you that is aware of what you have lived through. It's the awareness in the background that remains constant, never-changing, just there.

The conceptualized you that was created includes the name you were given, the values and morals you were taught, the personality you developed, the thoughts, beliefs and opinions you hold, the interests you became involved in, and much more. These are things you were not born with. Your body is part of you, but it is always changing. It does not look anything like what it was when you were 5 years old. Your body completely regenerates every 7 years, so physiologically you are not the same person (body) moment by moment.

Identity

A Transcendent Identity

The 'conceptualized self' (the self that people think they are) has many shortcomings and it causes a lot of fear and anxiety. When you think of 'yourself', it probably brings up a lot of negative thoughts about what you need to fix about yourself. Your mind says 'you' are a problem that needs to be fixed and that once your fix your shortcomings, you'll be happy. But this isn't true. Once you fix one thing, you notice something else that isn't good enough.

Transcendent means it transcends the person, going beyond the conceptualized self. On the surface level, every person has shortcomings. Become compassionate towards yourself, seeing that you are much more than your shortcomings. The shortcomings become less dysfunctional and cause less suffering the more you keep your attention on the deeper part of you, the 'real' you.

Perfection, or getting to the point in which a person has no more work to do on themselves and can't grow or evolve anymore isn't possible for human beings. There will always be opportunities to grow, things to learn, things that can be improved. The deeper you, the conscious you, is already perfect and complete. You don't need anything in order to become complete.

True identity vs conceptualized identity

The conceptualized identity includes a lot of negative, fearful thoughts which end up making us feel insecure, anxious, and afraid. Thought in itself is not problematic. Emotion is not problematic. Identification with thought and identification with emotion is problematic. When you become identified with thoughts it means the awareness behind the thoughts has been overshadowed so you get swept away by those thoughts and emotions. In those moments you act as if you ARE the thoughts instead of have thoughts.

The goal is to notice the thoughts but not to become identified with the thoughts (or emotions). This is not suppressing or denying, but just not becoming identified with it.

Staying present during an interaction is a vital skill. Don't become identified with what you are saying. Notice that what you are saying are just verbalized thoughts, and the key to presence is to not be identified with thinking. If you free your mind from identifications, your mind becomes a miracle.

Understanding Past and Future

Most people spend their time thinking about the past or worrying about the future. The past feels very real to most people, where is the past? Let's really take a look at this concept. A common answer that comes up is: the past is behind me. Look behind you right now. Where is the past? It's gone. Gone where? In the past. But where??? No where. It doesn't exist. If I offered to pay you 10 million dollars to go back to 1:00 pm yesterday, you couldn't do it. No matter how hard you tried, you'd realize that there is no where to get to because it doesn't exist. Once the moment passes, it's gone. We hold on to the concept of the past like it's a real place to get to, but it's nothing more than a concept.

The only time that ever exists is the 'now'. Our minds make the past feel like it's very real. A key point to making mindfulness work is fully accepting that the past is completely insubstantial because it is not real, it does not exist. Some people misinterpret this to mean denial of the past. This is not denial. This is just realizing what is is, and what isn't isn't. The now 'is' and the past 'isn't'. So when the past comes up, ask yourself if you really need to be thinking about that right now. More often than not, the answer is no.

The future has no existence except as a thought. Your mind believes it is something else, something real to get to and that once you get there, you'll be happy, or you'll finally love yourself or be okay with yourself. The hope is that at some point in the future, the problem of your 'self' will be resolved.

Losing control of your memory (past) and your imagination (future, anxiety).

The past does not exist unless you create a thought about the past. There is no past. And you can only think that thought about the past now. You can never access the past or the future, because they don't exist. Where are they? They are only thoughts. Time is a man made concept that only exists as a thought.

The link between past and future and mental health

Depression and anxiety are the most common mental illnesses in the world. When you think about distressing events that happened in the past, that's depression. In psychology we call it morbid rumination. You just relive the past experience over and over in your mind, wishing it had been different. This type of thinking has no impact on the actual events. It renders you powerless because you're spending mental energy trying to impact something that no longer exists. You can't change the past, but you can impact the now. Accept what happened, and ask 'what now?'. Acceptance does not mean you approve or even think it's okay, it just means acknowledging that what happened happened. It's saying yes to what happened. Saying no to what happened is torturous because we know it happened, but we're stuck wishing it hadn't happened. That is a sure way to suffer forever. Say yes to what happened. Take the judgment out of it (liking or disliking what happened). You can't move forward without acceptance.

The next question is, where is the future? The future feels very real to most people as well. But where is it? Again, only in our imaginations. We can only imagine the future, but we can't ever live in the future. Any distressing, worrying thought about the future is anxiety. Anxiety is worrying about what is not happening.

Although the concept of the future seems very real, the future only ever happens in the now. Try to get to 5 minutes from now. Even if someone offered you 10 million dollars to get to the future (5 minutes from now) you wouldn't be able to do it. When 5 minutes comes, you will experience it in the now. Never as the future. There is no real future. There's just the present moment. Just the now.

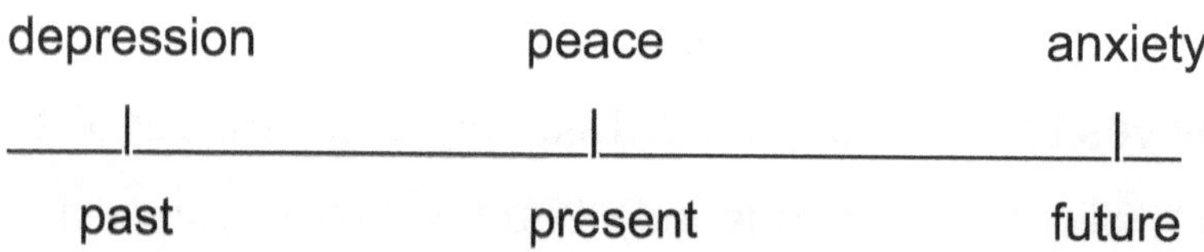

To recap, depression always involves past-based thinking. Ruminating about distressing thoughts about the past, thinking why did they do this, or why did I do that. Wishing it was different. Anxiety always involves future-based thinking.

Anxiety can vary from worrying about what will happen in a specific situation like planning a date and worrying that it will go wrong, saying something stupid at a business meeting, to more general thoughts like "my life is over", "I've ruined my life", "I will never be happy", "I'm a failure".

Past-based thinking involves your memory and future-based thinking involves your imagination. They are thoughts **not** focused on what is actually happening in the present moment reality. Reality only exists in the present moment. Thinking about past or future is unnecessary and often delusional.

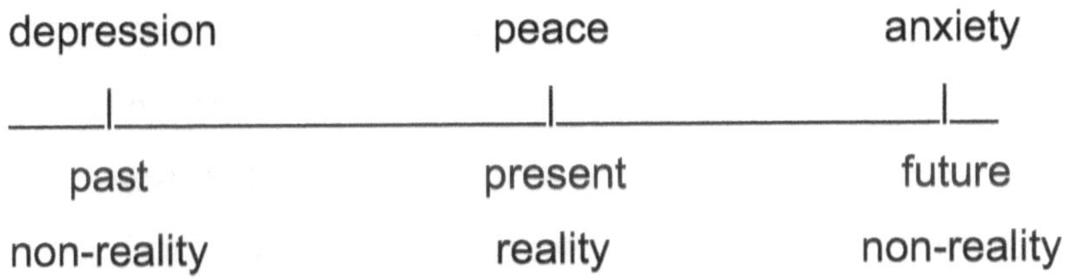

Make a commitment to only deal in reality. When distressing thoughts occur, do present moment reality checks to determine if you are dealing in reality or non-reality. Present moment reality checks include noticing where you actually are, what you are actually experiencing. For example: I'm sitting on a chair in my living room, the sun is shining through the window. The temperature is comfortable, I am safe.

Anxiety

Anxiety is a fear response in which we perceive a lack of physical or emotional safety. We experience the urge to fight, flee, or freeze. Every time we give in to the fear, it becomes stronger. We become afraid of being afraid, anxious about being anxious. The answer is: do not give in to the fear. When you give in to the fear (ex: you decide not to go to a party you really wanted to go to) you experience relief from the anxiety. However, because you experienced relief, the next time you are invited to a party it will be even harder to make yourself go because you reinforced the response that gave you relief (but it's the opposite of what you want).

Anxiety is fear of the future. You can't overcome what does not exist. Since anxiety is fear about the future, you can never overcome it because it doesn't exist. The fear exists in your imagination, but it's not actually in the world. How do you fight something that doesn't exist? Most of the things you've feared in the past never even happened. If thoughts are about the future, you can't do anything about it because it's not happening. That's why anxiety is so distressing: because you have no power to do something about something that isn't happening (non-reality).

You can only actually do something about things that are actually happening right now (reality). If there is something you can do, then take action now, and know that you've done all you can for now. Drop any other thoughts about it, recognizing that any worrying won't actually help you.

For example, you are worried that you can't pay a bill and you're going to have your electricity cut off at the end of the month. You worry, worry, worry. Ask yourself: is there anything I can do about it right now? You may be able to call the company and ask for an extension, you may be able to call a friend and ask if you can borrow the money, you may be able to pick up a side job to make some extra money. Those are actions you can take right now. Once you've done all you can, drop it. Notice that right now, you still have electricity. If it gets to the point where the worst case scenario has happened, the lights are cut off, then you will handle it at that time. Right now, the lights are on.

Life grants you the grace of one moment at a time. You don't have to worry about the rest of your life because life unfolds only in this moment. Can you handle this moment? Yes? Then you can handle your life. One moment at a time.

Planning

Does staying in the present moment mean that you can't plan for the future? Not at all! For practical purposes, planning and setting goals is beneficial.

How to plan: Just say you want to go to New York next month. You will need to make travel arrangements. You look at the calendar and select the dates. This part of the process requires planning into the future, which is completely appropriate. In the now, you may purchase your airline tickets and book your hotel. Then that's it. No more thinking is required. What often happens is you start worrying about it. What if I miss my flight, what if something goes wrong? That is the unnecessary thinking about the future that most people engage in. That's when you bring yourself back to the present moment and tell yourself, "I don't need to think about that right now, because it isn't happening."

Another example could be you decide to go back to school. Planning for the future is appropriate as you submit your application and select the courses you'll take. Then that's it. No more future is required. Just attend the classes when it's time to attend the classes. No worries about 'what if I don't pass, what if I'm not smart enough, what if I fail?' Bring yourself back to the present moment. Ask yourself if you need to be thinking about that right now.

The meaning of things

Life in and of itself is devoid of meaning. This is often a very difficult concept to grasp because we are so fiercely attached to the meaning we give life. Things happen. We create meaning. Nothing else. This notion can be very scary or very liberating. It can make us feel a sense of loss and insignificance, but it can open up a world of possibilities where there once were none.

For every single situation, something happens, and we construct a story about it. We even go a step further and make it mean something about us. For example: What happened: You go out on a date, the person doesn't call you back for a second date. The story: I'm being rejected. Something must be wrong with me. Meaning about me: I'm not good enough or I'm unlovable.

You carry the 'what I made it mean about me' around with you. You walk in to the next date with a belief that you're not good enough, which taints the experience. You try to not be found out that you're not good enough, so you try so hard to be good enough. The other person senses something's off with you, but they can't tell what it was. So they decide they don't want to go on a second date. The cycle repeats itself, thus reinforcing the negative core belief that you're not good enough.

Identity: Who are you?

Take a moment to ask yourself silently:

Who am I?

Sit with this question and see what comes up.

If you are not your thoughts, then who are you?

To get a sense of the real you, think back to experiences you had when you were 5 years old or 10 years old. You don't look anything like you did back then, but you know you were there, you lived those experiences. So if your body is different, what has remained the same? The one who is aware, the observer, the silent witness. The one who is aware is saying, "I have not gone anywhere. I am within you. Just look within and you will find me there."

Your mind-made identity is based in fear, so it is always on the lookout for threats to its survival. It will constantly be comparing itself to others, sizing others up to see if they are a threat or if they are 'less than' you.

In the absence of a real sense of identity, we create a fictional identity (a miserable identity, lots of drama). When you begin to see your own drama as an illusion, a fictional character, you will laugh and smile.

Why are most people unhappy?

Society is suffering from a loss of meaning, direction, vitality, mission, purpose, identity, and genuine connection. Most people experience a deep unhappiness that is considered ordinary. We may even start to believe that we've never been happy. But you weren't born unhappy. Children are naturally happy. Who do you know who is truly happy? Everyone's trying to be happy but no one is actually happy. Why?

Your mind might argue that you know lots of happy people. Some people are surface-level happy. They derive their happiness from external sources and when they obtain the new relationship, job, house, car, body, etc, they appear to be very happy. But this happiness is fleeting. Really stop and think about this. How many people do you know who are truly happy? Is their sense of happiness internally derived and not dependent on external conditions? If they lost the house, the car, the job, the relationship, what would they be like?

Break from the illusional traps of life

When I ask people what they want, the most common response is "I want to be happy," or "I just want to be okay". A common dialogue goes as follows:

Me: "Are you okay now?"

Other: "No".

Me: "But we're sitting in this room, you seem okay, right?"

Other: "Well yes, but I'm not really."

Me: "Why?"

Other: "Well because I need other people to make me happy, I need their approval."

Me: "If you just stay in reality, not focusing on what your mind is telling you, but focusing on what's actually happening, do you need anything from anyone right at this moment?"

Other: "No"

Me: "Are you okay right now?"

Other: "Yes".

Me: "So are you okay, really?"

Other: "Yes" (reluctantly, lol)

How you became who you are

What were you like at the age of 3? Picture yourself when you were 2 or 3 years old. If you have difficulty thinking of yourself, imagine your children or any children you've been around. What are they like? Some words that might come up are: carefree, happy, fully of life, energetic, spontaneous, adventurous, and free. They are honest, not concerned about self-image, they have no worries.

Children are naturally happy. We have to do something to make them unhappy, like make them go to bed or take away their toy. Even after something makes them unhappy, they forget about it and return to the happy state.

Adults are the opposite. Most adults live in a state of unhappiness and discontent and we have to do something to make us happy, like go on vacation, drink, use drugs, have sex, spend money, watch sports. These things distract us from the usual unhappy state. We experience momentary happiness then we're right back to being unhappy.

Think about most adults and teens you know. What words would you use to describe them or yourself? Some words might be: stressed, anxious, depressed, angry, unhappy, overworked, lonely. Adults are used to being in a state of unhappiness and complaining. Have you ever wondered when this changed for you? How did you go from being carefree, full of energy and vitality, to stressed, worried and unhappy?

You weren't born unhappy. What happened between childhood and adulthood to create such a shift? Children don't have concerns that adults have. Responsibilities. Although this is true, it's not the external circumstances that are at the root of our unhappiness. The true source of unhappiness comes from within. It's what you tell yourself silently day after day. The negative stuff you probably don't want anyone to know. Worries that you're incompetent, unlovable, a failure, or just plain bad. Worries that you can't trust others, fear of abandonment, fear of rejection. With thoughts like these, the world can seem like a dark and lonely place.

During a group session I facilitated, a man stated that depression is his natural state. I asked him when he first noticed this. He said "I've always been depressed".

It might seem that you've always been unhappy, but the unhappy self didn't exist when you were born. It was created by life experiences. Our natural state is joy. If you ever doubt this, just look at a 3 year old.

The creation of self

Little children are one with the world. They don't perceive themselves as separate from the rest of the world. That's what allows them to be spontaneous and free, dancing, jumping and singing without any concern about what other people think. They do things adults would never be able to do.

Then some time in early childhood, somewhere between the ages of 3 and 5, we have experiences in which we first experience ourselves as separate from the world. Before then, what made you be carefree and spontaneous was that you were one with everything. You did not see yourself as separate. You belonged. Once you began to believe you were separate, you created an identity whose motivation was to survive, to belong. Early childhood experiences began to shape the identity you created. Your mom criticized you, your dad left, you were made fun of in school, you were abused.

What ever happened to you made you believe something was wrong with you, and you had to fix it in order to get love and acceptance. You created a negative core belief (or several) because of these experiences. "I'm not good enough." "I'm bad." "I'm unlovable." "I'm unworthy." "I don't deserve love." "I'm a failure." You began to believe these things about yourself, that deep down you were just plain defective.

So then you developed strategies to compensate for these defects. I'll be smart enough, pretty enough, strong enough, funny enough, successful enough, popular enough, tough enough, sexy enough. I'll make you like me. The mind made identity is a false self you created for the sake of survival.

Once you experienced a separation of self and world, it was terrifying and you did not know what to make of it. You were little and you had to learn how to survive in this vast experience. You created an idealized version of yourself that you present to the world. This is the person you want people to believe that you are, and who you aspire to be. You want the world to believe you've 'got it together'. You engage in behaviors that increase your social capital.

You convey to others the ideals you aspire to portray with the things that you buy, the ideas and opinions you share and the groups you belong to. You signal to the world your values and ideals, your social class, religious views, political views, etc. You do and say what you think people want to see and hear for fear of being ostracized. The fear of not fitting in drives your behavior. You betray yourself in order to gain their acceptance. You are a prisoner. You are always thinking about how you appear to others, even when there are no others around.

Anxiety occurs when you perceive you may be rejected by them. We are all actors. The 'conceptualized self' is nothing more than roles and performances. You act out social scripts and performances in an effort to create a desired impression. When your concept of self comes under attack you go into survival mode. You freak out because you fear annihilation.

Your identity is wrapped up in people and things, titles and roles. The truth is, if the worst happens, you're not going to die. you'll still be okay. If they leave you, you lose the house, or they fire you, you'll still be okay.

If they laugh at you, they ridicule you, they break your heart, you lose the job…it's not going to kill you. If people laugh at you, so what? People thinking something about you doesn't make it true. You don't become crazy just because someone thinks you're crazy.

When did you stop loving yourself? When was the first time you noticed "I hate myself" or "I don't love myself"?

Who you really are

You are an expression of life itself. If you see reality as it is, you are life, just as trees, flowers, animals, and the earth are expressions of life itself, so are you. Your mind creates a concept called 'my life', but really to think that's who you are is to limit yourself in the most extreme way. It's like seeing a chrysalis and saying who you are is the cocoon and missing the magnificence of what's inside. You are not just the shell. You do not experience a life, you are life. You have an intelligence within, that makes your heart beat, that keeps you breathing, that makes every cell in your body operate.

At some level, you have always existed. Matter cannot be created or destroyed. You are energy, life force. The physical form changes, transforms, but you cannot disappear.

Your mind-identified self fights for survival, fears annihilation, but the truth is, you do not die. Nothing can ever destroy you.

Nothing has an ego. Plants, animals, flowers, rocks, trees, the moon, dirt, the sea have no ego. Even human beings have no ego. We are responding to something that's not really there. It's an imaginary identity we acquire, like actors on a stage. It's like you're watching a movie and interacting with a character on the movie screen. The person on the movie screen isn't really there. We act like it's real, but at the deepest level, it is not there.

When you are interacting with others, look beyond the imagined self-identity the person has created. It's not who they really are. It's a persona, an actor, a character they have created. The ego causes separation, but it's made up. It's an illusion and we're living like it's real. When we begin to see things clearly, we can see beyond the antics, beyond the noise and we realize that everything is sacred. When there is no ego, you have reverence for everybody and everything.

Getting to the source of who you really are, or self-realization is attained by discovering what you are not. You can never know by trying to find out what it is.

The real self is not your body, it is not your mind, it is not your thoughts, it is not your beliefs, it is not your personality, it is not your opinions. It is not any of those things. All of these things are either always changing and things you've acquired. Anything you acquire cannot be you. When you've gone through everything and there's nothing left, that's what it is. Nothing. Emptiness. Now, with that clean slate, with the emptiness as a starting point, you can engage in the world with a sense of ease and freedom, a playfulness, knowing that the real self is untouchable.

The real you can't be destroyed by the actions of others. Go deep and reconnect with the deepest part of you, the part that has just observed the pain. The part that remains strong and peaceful no matter what.

Why are you afraid? What can the world do to you? Nothing.

You can engage with the material world, with ideas, but you're not attached to them or identified with them. You are free.

Distraction

Almost everyone I've ever worked with reports feeling a sense of loneliness, emptiness, or unfulfillment that they just can't shake. Some have described it as a hollow feeling, a void, or an empty feeling. This issue must be addressed from existential perspective.

You may look around and think most people seem okay. This is because they create a surface-level happiness, a facade that masks their true pain. As previously mentioned, people attempt to avoid the emptiness inside by creating distractions.

We've developed socially acceptable ways of escaping reality. Watching television, social media, incessant use of phones, having sex, making money, getting in and out of relationships, overworking, shopping, watching sports, drinking, using drugs…all are ways in which people attempt to avoid stillness. They need to avoid stillness because the pain and emptiness is always there, just underneath the distraction.

As long as the distraction is there, they feel 'okay', but never really truly happy or at ease. They jump from one distraction to the next, the next degree, accomplishment, material possession, relationship, etc. You can never get enough of what you don't need. You get temporary relief but the emptiness is always there.

Thoughts can be used to create specific life situations that appear satisfying on the surface level. These things have no existential relevance, only psychological or social relevance. Caring about what others think of you has no existential relevance.

Stop trying to control your mind

If you are very identified with your mind, with your thoughts, you won't be able to quiet your mind. If you are identified with your body, your looks, your clothes, your age, your politics, your status, your money, your title, you will constantly worry about losing these things or becoming more thought these things, trying to enhance your sense of self through these things.

Try to create a little distance from the mind. Even if it's a noisy mind, it's still okay. Just notice the noise, disengage from identifying with all the thoughts.

You do this by bringing your full attention to the present moment. Noticing, being aware of what's actually happening now instead of thinking about future or past.

Once you disengage from the mind, you disengage from all identity, because the mind is the one who creates all the identities. Identity exists in past or future, but not in the now. Your identity is either what you know about yourself regarding past experiences or what you think you will become in the future. Your 'identity' doesn't exist in the now.

Where is the self that you refer to? If all your attention is here, there is no self. The 'self' dissolves and all that's left is pure awareness, true freedom. We want to look good in other people's eyes, we want to belong. We become concerned with consumerism in an effort to fit in. We aspire to be good enough. We are less connected with others. We engage in less meaningful interactions. "Making it" or "having it all" is not the answer. Think of the celebrities who have it all and are so unhappy they are plagued with addictions. Some find life so unbearable it brings them to the point of suicide. We need to re-humanize our lives. We need to shift from competition and comparison to cooperation and connection.

Becoming fully involved in life

When you no longer depend on the world to make you happy, you are able to become fully involved in life without fear of losing yourself when things don't go your way. Be fully involved, but not dependent on your relationships, your job, you looks, your material things to make you happy. Fear of getting attached leads to avoidance of life. You can't fully experience life if you're not involved.

Be involved fully in every aspect of life, even the simplest acts, and life will be extraordinary. Your perceptions become distorted when you become identified with something or someone. For example, when you become identified, defined by, your romantic relationship, it feels as if you'll die if they leave you. In reality, your life does not depend on this person choosing to be with you, but your perceptions are so distorted because you identify your 'self' with the relationship.

Don't create an identity out of anything outside of yourself. Stay rooted in your being, knowing you are whole and complete, then fully engage in the world.

Externally derived happiness

If you depend on external things and circumstances to make you happy, you will suffer. What brings you happiness today will bring you suffering tomorrow. It's okay to enjoy things, but if you do those things or have those relationships in order to be happy, that will lead to pain. If you become attached to those people or things for a sense of happiness, then you are at risk of crumbling when those things or relationships no longer exist. Find the happiness within before you engage in worldly pursuits. That way you can fully enjoy those people and things without the fear of the inevitable loss. Most people can't enjoy pleasant things once they obtain them because they are always afraid they will lose them. Become fully involved in life but don't derive your sense of self-worth or happiness from that involvement.

Everything emanates from your mind

Nothing that you experience ever happens outside of yourself. Everything that happens to you, happens within you. You can't experience anything 'out there'. It always happens 'in here'. Your perception shapes your reality. If you reflect on every experience you've ever had, what you saw, felt, thought, heard, perceived, it was always experienced from within you.

The realization that everything that appears is a manifestation of your mind is your liberation, because that means you have control over how you respond to your own experiences. Nothing outside of you is in your control. Only what is inside of you is in your control. This leads to another very important point: stop trying to control things outside of you.

Everything is fleeting

Life as we live it in human form is fleeting. Nothing lasts. We have expectations that things will last forever, like relationships, jobs, roles, titles, material things. None of these things will last forever. Loss is a part of life. Change is constantly happening. You will eventually lose everyone that you love, either through physical death, or the relationship will come to an end or the nature of the relationship will change (such as when children grow up and leave the home).

This realization allows us to fully appreciate our loved ones when they're in our presence because we understand that they won't always be there. When you're enjoying coffee with your partner, you'll be there fully, soaking in the moment, knowing one day he or she won't be there. When you're working, you'll understand that you won't always work there. When you're with your children you'll know that they will grow up and leave. When you're with your parents, you'll know they'll grow old and die. When you're engaged in physical activity, you'll recognize that one day, if you live long enough, you will get sick. You will lose your physical abilities. Everyone will die. You will die. There is no right age for someone to die. If you love that person, it will never feel like the right time.

Content vs. Context

Content versus context essentially refers to doing versus being. Many people find themselves doing all the 'right' things, but never really feeling happy or fulfilled. It's like they're going through the motions and still, things don't work out. "But I did what I was supposed to do!"

For example, you can read books and learn things about how to make relationships work, so you can get the content right, but if the context in which you take those actions is "I'm unlovable", "I'm unworthy" "I'm not good enough", it won't matter what you do. It still won't work. Information (content) is actually a small part of the equation compared to who you're being (context).

Who you're being, what you believe, the filter from which you live your life determines the outcome. Many of us focus on learning more, learning skills and going through the motions. If the context isn't addressed, it doesn't matter what you do or how much you know. You will always feel that something is lacking, a void, emptiness, unfulfilled, lonely. I can't stress this enough: until you get the context right, it won't matter what you do (content).

Shifting the context means focusing more on the human being instead of the human doing.

Human Being vs. Human Doing

You are a human being. The human part is the surface self and involves the mind and the body. The being part is the essential self, the part of you this is aware that you exist. Remain connected to the deeper self where you are in touch with your essential awareness, don't get lost in the doing, surface-level stuff.

Shifting perspective

Practice shifting perspective from what is seen (content) to who sees (context). Who is the seer? Who is the knower? Forget about what you see (the content) and focus on who sees (context). Do this with a beautiful, pleasant scene and forget about what you're observing. Focus on who is the observer - who is observing?

Unfulfilled expectations

A fundamental shift required for well-being includes seeing life as it is instead of how we think it should be. For the most part, people experience disappointment and frustration because they have expectations that life should be a certain way. That things should go a certain way, that 'bad things shouldn't happen to me' and they ask 'why is this happening to me?'. Once we begin to live life on life's terms instead of the delusional expectations humans place on life, we actually have a chance to be happy. We give up the expectations like "he should be with me forever", or "I should always be happy".

If you think about something you've ever been upset or unhappy about, it's likely you had an expectation that something or someone should have been a certain way. They weren't and you were disappointed. The only way out of this unhappiness is to identify what your expectation was and to drop it. You stop trying to change them and start taking responsibility for your unhappiness. I'm not unhappy because you got home late, I'm unhappy because I had an expectation that you'd be home in time for dinner. Then you can take empowered action from that stance.

If you cling to the complaint that your unhappiness stems from the other person's actions, you remain powerless because they may or may not adjust their behavior in the future. Take responsibility for your part and act accordingly.

Love is the answer for everything.

Love

Love, in it's purest definition means acceptance. It means another sees you as you are and accepts you fully. When you stand in judgment, you are saying that person is not acceptable. You are negating their humanity. Anytime you notice yourself judging, say thank you, because you are being given an opportunity to love. Don't waste time judging yourself because you were judging. Notice the judgment but don't attach any importance to it, don't act from the place of judgment. Notice what your mind is doing and disregard it.

Once you start being more present, you will notice just how much thinking you do and how much of it involves judgment. It may feel like you're always judging! So yes, your mind is always judging. Within seconds of seeing a person for the first time, you assess their social status, friendliness, etiquette, approachability, sexuality, religion, and how educated they are. You are essentially assessing how useful this person is to you. You use those judgments to determine the person's value. Is this person valuable to me? Can the person help me gain social capital?

Judge the situation or the experience, not the person. Don't diminish their humanity, just note if the situation works for you or not, or if your experience of being with the person energizes you or drains you.

If it works, great, if it doesn't work, no need to name call, criticize or put them down. Just acknowledge that the situation isn't workable for you and move on.

Your brain is hardwired to assess and judge situations in order to assess safety. Humans have the ability to assess emotional safety as well as physical safety. In this regard it is useful and necessary for our survival to employ judgment. Where things go awry is when we begin to judge people. They are this, he is that. She is this way, those people are that way. In this sense, every time we judge people, we limit our ability to connect with them deeply. There is no possibility for a healthy relationship when you have judged a person as being a certain way.

For example, if a person engages in unconscious behavior, you will say he is that way, even if he only did that once. He will always show up for you that way, not because he necessarily IS that way, but because you have put him in a box and won't allow yourself to see him any other way. Having said that, you have the right to choose who is in your life and who is not.

Attachment in Love relationships

Love and attachment are not the same. Attachment in this discussion is not the same as attachment theory. Attachment for the purposes of this conversation refers to a desperate clinging driven by a perceived sense of lack. When you are attached you become reckless because your behavior is driven by selfish motivations. You NEED the other person in order to feel happy and complete. Even if you do 'nice' things for the other person (content), the intention is based on selfishness, which can never be loving and ultimately harms the other person.

When there is attachment you are in a delusional state because your identity believes it's survival depends on the other person. Your madness is covered up until a situation arises that reveals the insanity. He doesn't call, you don't get the promotion. Your madness is exposed. The moment your actions are motivated by attachment they become lifeless. The context is scarcity and desperation. There is no energy or vitality, just a desperate clinging.

Nonattachment in Love

The source of love is always inside you. People come along and bring the experience of love into awareness, and we say we love them. Yes, good, but realize that you are the source of that love, and it can never leave you. They helped you recognize it, experience it, but they can't take it away from you. If you think they are the source of your love, you will cling to them and try to control them in an effort to keep them from ever leaving you. This is addictive attachment. They will feel trapped. True love liberates.

If you really love someone, you will feel that love whether they are next to you, a thousand miles away, and even when they've transitioned. People you love are just there to open your awareness up to that which is already in you. The more you love the more you'll find that you can extend that love to more and more people, until there is only love that emanates from you. You develop a certain reverence for everyone and everything. Who you really are is love, which at it's basic form is just full-acceptance; the absence of judgment.

True love can never leave you. If you love someone, even after the relationship ends (they no longer choose you or through physical death), you will still feel their love.

The reverence for them remains, and you still wish the best for them.

Don't depend on anyone in order to express the love that is you. You be loving of your own volition, not because of somebody else. Don't expect anyone to make you happy. Don't make someone else responsible for making you feel love. See things as they really are. Everything you experience happens within you, not outside of you. You are responsible for the love that you feel. If you want love in a situation, bring love. Be loving. Don't expect anyone else to create that experience for you. It's up to you. This is one of the most liberating shifts that a person can experience.

Love and relationships

Love and relationships are not the same thing. You can love someone and not be in a relationship with them. And you can be in a relationship with someone and not love them. Love is acceptance of the other as they are. This can be very difficult when people live together in a domestic partnership.

To make a loving relationship work, both people have the intention and capacity to offer joy and happiness to one another. The paradox is that you don't expect it from the other, but if the other offers the same to you, it works! The key is to not EXPECT it from the other, but have a mutual understanding that you both intend to offer joy and happiness.

Recognizing that life is painful, you understand that everyone carries some emotional pain. You strive to alleviate and transform their suffering when it emerges. This requires having a deep concern for the other person. You offer reassurance to one another. You say "no matter what, I'm here". "We will get through this."

Engage with the intention to maintain mental calmness and to respond to each other with love especially in difficult situations. This requires seeing the person as your partner, not your enemy. Remain in a state non-attachment.

Remember, if your love has attachment or clinging in it, it is not true love. When you love something, you become one with it. Become one with your partner. Become one with your children. Become one with your family, your friends, your community. Become one with nature. Become one with everything. Love everything. If you have expectations of people, sooner or later they will disappoint you.

A daily exercise to keep you grounded in reality is to remind yourself that you don't need other people for your survival. You switch the context from beggar to one who is whole and complete and is there to offer love instead of needing to get, get get. Say to yourself silently: I don't need you in order to exist. Then and only then are you truly able to offer unconditional love. A space of freedom moves in and then your interactions will come from a context of true love, not of desperate clinging or addictive need. Focus on what you have to offer instead of what you need to get.

Others can only love you to the capacity that they love themselves. The same is true for you. You can't give what you don't have. You can only love to the capacity that you love yourself.

Reflections on Relationships

If you've had relationships that you don't perceive as positive, ask 'what was this person here to teach me?' Once you learn the lesson, accept the lesson and move on. Some people come into your life to awaken you from some false reality you've created. Their purpose was to help you open your eyes. Then they leave. No relationship lasts forever. Don't lament the amount of time you had with someone and don't stay in something you shouldn't stay in just because you've invested so much time. Accept the impermanence of all relationships.

Anyone who is okay with you being miserable so that they can be happy does not really love you. Your mind might want to go a step further and judge them as 'bad' people. That's not necessary. All that is required is that you see things as they are.

Liking Yourself

If you don't like you, what makes you think other people are going to like you? It's funny how people will dislike themselves so much, but then they expect everybody else to love them. Why would somebody like you if you don't even like yourself?

Loving Yourself

Loving yourself is better than hating yourself, but ultimately you want to move away from identifying with thoughts and opinions about how lovable/unlovable you are, because that's just more activity of the mind-made, conceptualized self. If you observe other sentient beings, like dogs, cats, horses, cows, birds, they just are who they are. They are not concerned with loving themselves. They don't have a self-image. They don't have opinions about themselves at all. Let go of having your self-image define who you are. Who you are is the presence behind the thoughts of 'who you think you are'. Just be who you are. Stop needing to define it. Focus on *being* love instead of trying to prove you are lovable.

Stop relating to yourself as somebody who is deprived of love. When you interact with others from the context of deprivation, it robs the both of you of authentic connection.

When you think you need something from someone else, you become a beggar, always trying to get something (appreciation, validation, acknowledgment). And it's never enough. They end up feeling depleted and you end up feeling empty and cheated.

Try to love yourself as much as you want someone else to. Whatever you want from someone else, give it to yourself.

What to do if you can't love yourself

Sometimes you may be so trapped in self-loathing that you feel you couldn't love yourself even if you tried. Sometimes your mind blocks the ability for you to feel the love that is already in you.

If you find you can't love yourself, think of someone you love. This will allow you to immediately access the love that is already inside you.

Compassion for Self

"If your compassion does not include yourself, it is incomplete." - Buddha

You can't give what you don't have. Fill yourself with love, be kind to yourself, take care of yourself. Be full of love, full of compassion, full of joy so that you can give that to others. Don't be ashamed of being the greatest version of yourself. This doesn't mean being arrogant, but being kind and peaceful. It's okay to be full of yourself - full of love, joy and peace! Be very careful about what you fill yourself up with, because that will be what you offer to others. If you are full of anger, resentment, guilt, or shame, what can you possibly offer those you love?

You can't hide what's inside you, because that's what you pour out. If you don't have love and compassion in you, people will feel it. Even if you do 'nice' things for them, it will be tainted by the negativity you have inside.

Extending compassion to yourself is vital for well-being. Many people say they love others but they don't extend that love to themselves. If you are committed to creating a loving, peaceful world, you have to stop being abusive, unloving, and hateful towards yourself. Whatever energy you are generating, whether it's towards yourself or others, is making the world more loving or more hateful.

It's healing the world or creating more suffering in the world. Make a promise that you will create no more suffering and hate in this world. Extend the love and compassion to yourself.

Compassion for others

Compassion means understanding the another person's pain. Compassion doesn't mean 'being nice'. Sometimes the most compassionate action will generate hostility on the part of the other person because you are no longer enabling them. They won't like it. They may say you're being mean; you're not being nice. Compassionate action does not mean punishment. It comes from a place of deep care and concern for the person's well-being.

Sometimes our desire to be liked and accepted will lead us to do things that are not in the best interest of our loved ones. For example, the parent who allows their drug addicted child to live in their home. The parents provide food shelter and the child continues to feed his addiction. The parents will say, "I can't throw him out in the street!" The reality is if the child isn't given consequences, the addiction will end up killing him. The parent would rather have that than have the child mad at her or for others to think she's a bad mom for throwing her son out of the house. The most compassionate action would be to offer food and shelter while the child gets sober, but to not allow him to continue to use drugs while he lives in the home. If he does, he has to go.

If he is able to feel the consequences of his actions, this may motivate him to seek help. The parents must understand that it's his choice. They are only enabling him to kill himself if they let him stay and continue to use drugs.

What's often at the root of this decision is parental guilt, avoiding conflict, and fear of what others will think about them. Love says: I'm here for you, the door is open, but I won't help you destroy yourself. Stay true to yourself. Sometimes being compassionate means the other person won't get what they want. That is okay.

If you believe somebody cares about you, you can go a long way.

That is why it is so important to show your children and loved ones that you care. Don't assume they already know. Tell them and show them.

Manipulation masked as caring

Coming clean about manipulative behavior is vital for healthy relationships. People manipulate others in an attempt to have their desires fulfilled. You want your partner to be a certain way. You want your children to act a certain way. You don't want them to make you look bad. This means treating others as objects to be controlled and manipulated in order for them to serve the purposes we want them to serve. When you are trying to get something from someone, you're not able to recognize their humanity. That's a strong statement, but really, you are so focused on getting what you want that you're not thinking about what they want. You may totally disregard their thoughts and feelings. It makes true connection impossible. It's an isolating experience because true connection isn't possible when there's an agenda.

Have roles, but don't get trapped in those roles. The predicament of most parents is they get trapped in their role and they get trapped in seeing their child in the child's role. They get so caught up in making sure they are seen as 'good' parents, that they lose focus on the fact that the child has their own journey, their own thoughts and feelings. They compromise the relationship.

How to become someone people actually want to be around

Listen

Most people aren't being present during a conversation. They either have their attention elsewhere or are thinking about what they are going to say next. Stay quiet when someone is talking. Then, when the person is done speaking, wait a second before responding. They might not be done yet. This helps to assure that you are responding to what they said instead of what you were going to say . If you are thinking of a response while they are talking, then you aren't listening to them.

People subconsciously know when you are not listening to them. They may talk, but they won't feel heard. You don't have to agree with what they are saying, but the relationship will be strengthened because they feel heard.

Stop Complaining

Nobody wants to hear your complaints. Complaining comes from a context of powerlessness because it has no impact; it doesn't change anything. It just makes people annoyed with you. The reason people become so annoyed with complainers is because there's no empowered action behind the words, so the complaints persist. Complaining changes nothing; alters nothing.

Most people don't really get how useless complaining is. To get a sense of how much impact your complaints have on the world, sit in a room with an empty chair in front of you. Complain away. Tell the chair what you're upset about. Tell it how you feel about things, your opinions, what you like, what you don't like, what people should do, and what they shouldn't do. Notice the response the chair has to your complaints.

Some people complain as if they expect the world to come to a screeching halt because they're upset about something. Life doesn't care that you're unhappy in your relationship. It just keeps going whether your relationships work or they don't work. And nobody cares that you don't like your boss. Life doesn't stop because something bad happened to you as a kid.

Life doesn't stop because your partner left you or because you got sick. Life will just keep going whether you're happy or not. It's up to you to take action to make it better, but complaining does nothing.

Become the Source of Solutions

In any given situation you can either be the source of problems (and complain about the problems), or you can be the source of solutions. If you are known as the source of solutions everyone will want to be around you. No one wants to be around people who are viewed as the source of problems or who just sit around complaining about problems. Wherever you go, be a solution. Be accountable.

Complaining reinforces the victim identity. You strengthen the victim identity by constantly talking about and thinking about how bad things are, how terrible your life is, how bad you've had it. It's fueling unhappiness, which drives people away.

Sometimes, you are impacted or directly affected by another person's hurtful behavior. Although you did not cause the pain, you are responsible for picking up the pieces and healing yourself. Your responsibility is to make conscious choices.

Be courageous enough to change it or fully accept the situation, but don't complain about it. Remaining in a helpless, complaining state has no impact and will never give you what you want. When you make conscious choices, you receive conscious consequences.

I'm not suggesting you always have to be happy about the situation. Everyone feels down sometimes. It's important to recognize when you're stuck in the negativity and have created an identity out of it. You have control over your life. You're not helpless.

When You Become Reactive

You're a human being and sometimes you're going to blow it. You'll say or do something in a moment in which you've lost touch with presence and have slipped back into your old patterns. Have Compassion for yourself. Instead of beating yourself up, just notice it and say "Oh, there it is again. I'm doing it again." Then just come back to the present moment.

On "Letting Go"

Sometimes we struggle with persistent thoughts about something painful that happened in the past. Well-meaning people will often advise us to just 'let it go'. If this gives you relief and you can just drop it, then great. But what happens when you can't let it go? Then on top of the thing that's distressing you, you start to feel bad about yourself. You think you're weak because others are able to 'let things go' and you can't. You think 'there must be something wrong with me because I can't let it go'. At this point, drop all attempts to let it go. There's no such thing as "letting it go" in your mind. What are you letting go of?

In these situations, letting go is just an idea that never happens. If you find yourself in the position of not being able to let something go, I would invite you to not let it go. Give up trying to let it go. Free yourself of that concept. Instead of moving away from it (let it go), turn towards the pain and begin to explore it. Move deeply into the exploration of the thing you can't let go of. What were the expectations you had? What are you hurt about? Acknowledge the pain instead of trying to 'let go' of the fact that there is pain.

As far as what to let go of, if there's any idea of retaliation or revenge, definitely let go of that.

Ways of letting go or avoiding ever getting to the place where you feel the need to let go:

Notice that you are here but you are wanting to be over there, whether that be in a physical space or emotional space. The pain comes from not wanting what actually is. You are still wanting to be in a relationship that no longer is: 'can't let go'. You are wanting what happened (somebody hurt you) to never have happened: 'can't let go'.

Freedom is wanting to be where you are. Begin to foster a sense of contentment with what actually is. Why? Because that's what *actually is.* Fighting with what actually is causes tremendous suffering and turmoil. The situation is probably painful enough as it is. You don't need to add to it. Learn to see what you can be at peace about in your current situation.

Making Right Choices

Every choice will either enhance your life or drain it. When your life choices harm you, it's an indication that you've got to change course. Don't betray yourself by staying in situations that cause you harm. Betrayal of the self is the worst type of betrayal. It hurts when others betray us, but there's nothing worse than betraying yourself. How do you know if the situation is right? You feel energized. You might feel tired, but you don't feel drained or depleted. You feel at peace even when things are challenging. If you are not at ease or if you find yourself in a constant state of confusion, it is not for you. If something or someone is right for you, you won't feel like you have to compromise your integrity or change who you are in order to fit in.

Making requests

When you make a request ,remember that the other person has the freedom to say no. If you make a request with the expectation that the person will say yes, and then they say no, you get mad. All it means is that the other person never really had a choice. It means you're attempting to control the other person's behavior. If they don't do what you want, there will be consequences. If the other person doesn't really have the choice to say no, be honest about it from the start. Don't ask as if it is a request. That's manipulative. Clearly state what it is: an expectation.

A request is, "can you please take out the trash?" The person has the freedom to say yes or no. A command is: "take out the trash, please". That indicates that there is an expectation that the person will do it.

Anger

Everybody feels angry sometimes. Anger is such an intense energy and many people were never taught how to manage it. Some people might think "I shouldn't feel angry". Don't judge yourself for feeling angry. If you feel angry, it means you're human. That's as far as it goes. Everything else is made up. You're not bad, or messed up or whatever your mind might be saying. You're just hurt and scared. It's your responsibility to heal, but don't judge yourself as defective because you feel angry. Many people are scared of their anger. It can be the most difficult emotion to regulate and many of us were never taught how to regulate it. Some of us explode and some of us hold it in. Lots of us have unresolved anger and we become explosive not because of the situation right in front of us, but because the situation activates some previous experience that's unresolved and that we feel really angry about.

Once you've resolved the past hurts that you're really angry about, you'll be able to respond to what's right in front of you, which is usually no big deal. If you are able to sense the anger coming, try to explain your anger instead of letting it build to the point you blow up. Sometimes the activation is too quick, and you're gone. The best thing to do at this point is to wait.

Don't say anything or do anything until the intense wave of anger subsides. This will usually only take a few minutes. Think of your mind as a snow globe, when you shake it (like when angry or excited), it's cloudy and you can't think clearly. But if you don't act, just be still and watch it settle, the intense energy dissipates and you're able to respond in a more productive way.

Once your executive functioning has returned, then you can explain your anger by stating that you feel anger because someone said or did something that you found hurtful or insensitive. "I feel angry that you didn't call to let me know you wouldn't be home in time for dinner. I waited until the food was cold. I felt disrespected." Then make a request: "From now on please call me to let me know not to wait for you." Once you have clearly communicated your request, it is up to the other person to honor the request or not. If they don't then the ball is back in your court. Will you drop your expectation that they call and let you know, accept that sometimes they won't call, or will you leave the situation?

Channel the energy of your anger towards something positive. Direct your anger towards what you care about, using that energy to impact positive change. Let it motivate you for good.

Honoring your truth

Pretending is for the movies. Real life requires the truth.

Trust yourself. When something is right, it will feel right. When something is wrong, it feels wrong. Don't allow anyone to disrespect you, manipulate you, or to treat you badly, whether it be your partner, your mother, your father, your sister, your brother, or your boss. You have the right to protect yourself and say no. If you don't feel like you can speak up because you are afraid of the consequences, think about how unhealthy that is. You have no voice in that relationship.

A healthy relationship allows for you to speak up and not be afraid that they will leave you, reject you, criticize you, abandon you, or hate you. If you self-censor for fear of their response, you are in an unhealthy relationship.

Practice: From this point forward, make a promise to yourself that you won't ever allow anyone to treat you badly, to manipulate you, to guilt you, or to disrespect you.

People might be better than you in some things but they are not more important than you. No one is more important than anyone else.

Beyond anxiety and depression

One of the most exciting discoveries of neuroscience is neuroplasticity - you can rewire your brain. You can create new neural connections and generate new thought patterns. Every single time you intercept a negative thought pattern, you are creating new neural connections. Don't be discouraged when you blow it. Just recommit to intercepting the negative thoughts that keep you anxious and depressed.

Practice focusing attention on new thought patterns that support your well-being. You can become resilient and you can strengthen thought circuits that support resilience by doing continuous present moment awareness checks throughout the day, meditating, spending time in nature and becoming still as often as possible.

Talk therapy can be useful for processing your pain and weakening some of the stubborn negative thought patterns that make mindfulness so difficult sometimes.

Worry

What to do instead of worrying:

1. Identify what you want or what the issue is that needs to be addressed

2. Identify factors you can control and factors you can't control

3. Focus your attention on factors within your control and take action

4. Don't allow yourself to focus your attention on factors outside of your control. As soon as you notice your mind going there, intercept the thought and redirect your attention to the factors you can control, or drop the situation entirely. Tell yourself silently, "I've done all I can for now and I'm not going to continue thinking about it right now".

Take care of yourself

Take care of your body, not out of vanity, but because your body is your vehicle. You want it to be in the best condition to take you where you need to go. Eat well, with the intention of nourishing your body. Enjoy your food and make eating a celebration. Break bread with others.

Include movement as part of your daily routine. Exercise doesn't have to mean going to the gym. It can be yard work or going for a walk.

Stay away from negative people. Surround yourself with positive people who exude energy and vitality. Maintain a sense of wonder and curiosity. Try new things and explore new places. Travel whenever you are able. See the world beyond your daily route. Discover how other people live.

Allow yourself to experience things that you enjoy. This could include taking a bubble bath, going for a walk or eating at your favorite restaurant—this practice reinforces the belief that your are worth it. No matter what your financial situation is, find ways to enjoy pleasant experiences and to enjoy life. Don't feel guilty.

Create a powerful intention for your life, a definite chief aim. What you actually decide to make of your life is up to you. There is no 'right' answer. It's only about what's right for you.

What's right for you may not be what's right for your parents, friends, colleagues. You don't have to do what they want. They have their own lives to live and you have yours. If they love you, they will be happy for you as you pursue your passions, even if it's not what they would choose.

Trust

Most of us want to trust others fully, but we're fearful about it. We're told that healthy relationships require us to fully trust, but when we try, we often have a strong visceral response against it. The reason you're having that response is because human beings are unpredictable. Even if their patterns are mostly predictable, at some point people will disappoint you.

At any given moment, people's sensibilities vary depending on the situation. Someone who is typically thoughtful may suddenly say something that you perceive as insensitive. You then focus on that one moment of insensitivity and you decide that this person can't be trusted. The person lied or said something insensitive to you, and that moment becomes a permanent fixture in your mind and you decide that is who they are.

Even if they display thoughtful behavior at other times, you won't be able to see it. You become trapped by this delusion. It's very important to understand that you are the one who is trapped by the delusion. If you give up the expectation that they should be constant and predictable, you can free yourself and open up to the possibility of having authentic, connected relationships with others.

Real trust can only exist at the level of being. People will say and do things you don't like, but there is always a human being behind that behavior. Don't equate what they do with who they are. Don't create an identity for them out of their moments of insensibility. Don't expect them to say and do the right thing or to be consistent in their behavior.

In order to respond effectively in life, you have to understand what you're dealing with. The world is insane. People are unconsciously responding to fearful thoughts. They are in survival mode; they fear annihilation, too. In order for you to be well, it's vital that you understand what you are dealing with. People are often wonderful and then something happens that activates them and they go crazy for a little while. Then they come back.

These moments of madness are not 'who they are'. Don't expect everyone to always do the 'right' thing. You might say, 'Well, I never would have done that.' Good. But what does judging them do? Does letting them know how much better you are than them actually help anything?

In order to respond effectively you have to assess each situation individually. There is not always a set response for each situation. You have to assess each situation with presence and attention, in order to be effective. Someone might seem trustworthy, but the truth is you can't ever know 100% that that person won't say or do something in the future that you find hurtful. People tell you to trust and so you fight your intuition and give them the benefit of the doubt. Then one day they don't keep their word. They've violated your trust. Most people will eventually let you down, either intentionally or unintentionally. That's the nature of human relationships.

The key to the concept of trust is this: adjust your expectations. Violations of trust occur when others don't meet our expectations. You can trust, but don't derive your sense of self from other people. Don't depend on them for your happiness and well-being. Understand human beings are often not trustworthy and most people will eventually disappoint you.

Since you don't ever know 100% what others will do, it's necessary to fully trust yourself. Trust that you will respond in the healthiest way possible to whatever situation arises. Promise not to betray yourself for the sake of keeping someone in your life. Stay in the moment, and if things are going well, great. But if things become unhealthy, trust that you will not go against your own self in order to preserve the relationship.

Bitterness and dissatisfaction result from people or situations not meeting your expectations. Since you can't control anything outside of yourself, you must control your expectations.

Victim/Not Victim

When painful experiences occur, it is normal for the system to take a little time to heal. You might be in shock, you might feel sad, angry, etc. This is normal. It becomes problematic when we begin identifying our sense of self with the distressing event. People will often use phrases like 'I'm broken' or 'I'm damaged' that indicate they've become identified with their pain. Someone not identified with their pain will accept that a painful experience has happened to them, but it doesn't alter their value or their sense of self.

One of the less subtle ways we become identified with our pain is to become a 'not victim' about it. You may have heard some people say 'I refuse to be a victim about this' and they may even take on advocacy work in order to 'fight' being victimized. We have to be very careful because although some people truly are not identified with the pain, and therefore are not victims, many people remain victims by fighting to not be a victim. Although they present differently than someone who has taken on the victim identity, (helpless, defenseless, weak, not capable of moving on because such and such happened) they are still 'owned' by the event. They are not free. It's got them.

They fight, are defensive, and their actions are dictated by making sure they're not victims. It's a different side of the same coin: still a victim.

This concept, that everything you fight, everything you resist has you, extends to all other areas of life. The adult who swears they will never be their parents is not free to be the parent they truly are, but is held hostage by trying to not be their parents. There is no freedom there.

Stop hiding

Most people hide because the context they operate from is: 'you are defined by what you do or by what happens to you'. Shift the context to: you are NOT defined by what happens to you or by what you do.

If the context is 'you are not defined by what you do or by what happens to you', then you won't need to hide. What happened is not who you are. It's just something that happened. No matter what you ever did or what was ever done to you, you get to decide to live a life worth living today. You get to be at peace today. You are so much more than what you did or what happened to you. Stop hiding.

Desire and Lust

"People are distracted by objects of desire, and afterwards repent of the lust they've indulged, because they have indulged with a phantom and are left even farther from Reality than before. Your desire for the illusory is a wing, by means of which a seeker might ascend to Reality. When you have indulged a lust, your wing drops off; you become lame and that fantasy flees. Preserve the wing and don't indulge such lust, so that the wing of desire may bear you to Paradise. People fancy they are enjoying themselves, but they are really tearing out their wings for the sake of an illusion." ~Rumi

"The most miserable mortals are they that deliver themselves up to their palates, or to their lusts; the pleasure is short, and turns presently nauseous, and the end of it is either shame or repentance." ~Lucius Annaeus Seneca

"The prison of lust is just that very one of which the soul shuts the doors upon herself; for each act of indulgence is the shooting of a fresh bolt." ~Plato~

Lust is an incredibly strong and powerful energy. When a person does not reign in the power of their sexual energy, their actions can be very careless and even dangerous. Learn to take responsibility for your sexual energy by practicing restraint, being mindful enough to not give in to destructive urges. Transmit that powerful energy into something positive. If you focus all your energy in the direction of something purposeful, the results will be extraordinary.

Finding your purpose

Your main purpose is just to be alive. Just exist. No agenda. When you are yourself, you will be amazed how the universe takes care of you. You don't have to force anything. What is meant for you will come.

You want to focus on life enhancing versus lifeless motivations. Life enhancing motivations include love and compassion. Lifeless motivations include trying to look good in the eyes of others, trying to get recognition and validation. Let your actions be motivated by things that make you feel alive. Be careful about trying to become virtuous or trying to be a 'good person', a 'nice person', in an effort to improve your self image or public image, so that others may think you're virtuous, good, or nice. This is another form of inauthenticity. It's your mind-made identity that longs to be somebody, to be viewed a certain way.

Only when you experience a shift in perception of self can you be truly virtuous, and in that case you're no longer concerned with how others view you, nor are you concerned with enhancing your self image. You become naturally virtuous with no effort at all.

Fear of being thought of as crazy or that there's something wrong with you

People who follow their own guidance instead of following the ideas and conditions that society lays out for them are often labeled crazy. It makes others feel uncomfortable when you follow your truth, so they may try to pathologize you. They'll say something's wrong with you. You don't fit in.

Trust yourself. Take care of yourself. Do no harm. Others may have a distorted view of who you are. Stay on your journey and trust yourself.

They've told you not to be emotional, not because they meant you harm, but because it's uncomfortable for them. They've been taught it's not okay to be emotional, to feel their emotions. Like its a sign of weakness. But they are wrong. The only way to wellness is to feel. It's not wrong to feel. You're a human being, not a robot.

Most people live in realities determined by others, by systems of education, religion, politics, and other authorities. Everyday affairs are largely dictated by 'looking good'. You won't look good anymore. You'll have to drop that in order to be free.

Getting past a bad childhood

"What if I was raised in a crazy environment? Doesn't that mean there's something wrong with me? How can I ever be okay? "

Living in insane circumstances as a child does not mean you are insane. Separate the situation from your identity. The situation might have been crazy but that doesn't mean that you are crazy. Don't identify your circumstances or situation as who you are.

Trust that you can heal

When you cut yourself, your body instantly begins to heal itself. Your mind has a self-healing mechanism as well. There are times when events are so distressing that we don't initially know what to do with the information. This is especially true of childhood trauma or distress. We end up with unresolved issues. It takes awareness in order to resolve those issues.

When you become aware of your pain and fear, you can begin the process of healing it. It is the same self that creates the fear, hides from it, then heals from it/resolves it. The healer is not outside of you. You are the healer and the one who needs healing.

It's Never Too Late

If you live one day fully and completely, that in itself is sufficient because one day contains everything, all of life. Most people don't know the experience of living a single day of complete joy and contentment. They are crippled with anxiety and depression. No matter how old you are, it's never too late.

Remove time from your suffering

Sometimes the present moment is very painful. Practice removing time (past and future) from your suffering. You may experience a heaviness or tension in your body in the present moment. Don't think about it. Don't add a story to the physiological sensations you are experiencing. Don't add thoughts to it. Just experience the sensation.

When feeling emotionally overwhelmed

Bear non-judgmental witness to your emotions when you are feeling emotionally overwhelmed. Don't beat yourself up or say, 'I shouldn't be feeling this way'. Take the judgment out of the experience.

Avoiding traps and pitfalls

Once you begin to have awareness, your ego will begin to identify you as enlightened, awake, special, and better than others. That's just more of the same pattern of identifying with thoughts and beliefs. Be careful to not identify yourself as enlightened and stay in the reality of what life is: ever-changing relationships and processes.

Nothing stays the same, so to claim that you are enlightened is to claim a fixed way of being, which is just another delusion. Instead of focusing on being an enlightened person, focus on enlightened activity. We are all just processes moment by moment having experiences, nothing is fixed and there is no fixed self. If you look inward and try to find 'you', you will realize that there is no you there, just a continuous flow of thoughts, emotions, actions. There are continuous changes but no fixed self.

When you give attention to the present moment and listen to sounds, you can't distinguish a boundary between the person listening to the sound and the sound itself. There's just awareness of sound. There is no "person" listening to the sound. There is just the sound being experienced. So ultimately that's all there is. There is awareness but there's no fixed "self" that you can perceive listening to the sound. Listen to the sounds in the room right now and notice if you can find the boundary between the sounds and the person or "self" listening to the sounds. There's just sound. Where is the self? There is just awareness of the sound.

Practice and Reflections

Stop Wanting

In order to truly live an authentic life, you have to know that you are whole and complete already. You don't need anything in order to make you complete.

Practice: try to not want anything from anyone or any situation.

"I don't want anything from ________."

"I don't want anything from this experience."

Sometimes you think you need someone's approval or you need a certain status in order to feel validated. Say:

"I don't need anything from ________."

Reflection: Who am I?

What element of myself can't be removed from me? What aspect remains present throughout my ever-changing experiences?

Awareness Check

Practice just being here in the moment, just being alive. Ask yourself silently: Am I aware? Take a moment before you answer. The space in between the thoughts is awareness. The question and the answer are thoughts.

Reflection:

If the voice in your head is you, then who is the one listening to it?

The self is a socially constructed illusion.

Be true to life by being true to this moment.

Living authentically requires that you be true to this moment. Be fully here, fully aware of what actually is. That is how you can be true to yourself and to others.

The real you:

Your body is not yourself. You refer to it as 'my body'. Who is the 'my' that you're referring to? If the body was you, why would you say 'my' body? You are the one who is aware of the body and the mind. You are awareness.   Throughout the day, ask yourself: Am I Aware?

Practice Feeling that You're Alive

Hold your attention to the aliveness of your body. If you're not yet able to feel the aliveness of your entire body, then notice the aliveness of your hands and hold your attention there. Hold, hold. Then begin to notice things around the room.

Personality: personality is rooted in fear and unworthiness. Personality is created, but it is not who you truly are.

Reflection: Running Away from Yourself

Why are people always trying to run away from themselves?
Why don't people want to be alone with themselves? Be-
cause they are always thinking. They don't want to be alone
with their thoughts. They need a distraction from the thinking.
Instead of distraction, practice being alone with yourself.
Be the awareness behind the thoughts and emotions.

Practice:

When interacting with others, ask yourself: "What is it that
really matters here?"
It's not about what you say but your level of consciousness
during the interaction.
Be careful not to get swept away by the need to be right, the
need to impress, the need for validation.

Reflections on Relationships

At any point in any relationship, you are either moving towards connection or disconnection.

What would have to happen for you to be satisfied in your relationship?

Give with no expectation of return.

Guilt

Guilt is a wasted emotion. Instead of feeling guilty, replace the guilt with taking responsibility and making conscious choices. Learn from the experience and focus on how you're being now. If you were dishonest in the past, but you are honest right now, focus on that. That is your redemption.

Living Powerfully

We look to the future in hopes that things will be different, but until we actually **do** something differently, there is no hope.

From now on, don't wait for something to happen to you. Take responsibility for making things happen.

Growing in Awareness

Becoming happy requires growth in awareness. You can grow in knowledge up to a certain point, but mostly you will grow in awareness. Every time you practice mindfulness, you are growing in awareness. You may gain a little more knowledge, too, but focus on being more aware, more awake.

Becoming Free

You don't have to do anything to be free. There is no process you have to undergo. You are free now. All that is required is to stop all effort, stop 'trying' to be happy and free and be still now. Quiet the mind and realize that you are already free.

The prison of other people's opinions

As long as other people's opinions matter more than your own, you are not free. You are owned by them. Set yourself free.

Practice: Free yourself of mental concepts

What is the sky?

Reflect on this for a moment. Your mind is probably very certain it knows what the sky is. It's very certain there is a sky.
Where is it?
Up there.
If you try to get the sky, you'll notice you can't.
If you go up to the sky, when will you get there? Where will you be?
If you went up, you'd just keep going and going until you're outside the boundaries of what we call earth, but you would not be able to determine where the sky ends.
You can't get the sky.
The sky is a mental concept. It's not necessarily real. It's a mental concept human beings accept as 'real'.

Practice not labeling or conceptualizing anything. Look at things without classifying or comparing them to something else.
Look at people and practice doing the same thing.

Practice: Become Renewed

Tonight as you go to sleep, let the past die. Don't wake up as the same one who went to bed the night before. Awaken as someone new. Drop the past. You don't need it. Let the one who is always renewed awaken in the morning.

Practice: Challenging negative core beliefs

The fixed self is an illusion. When you have negative core beliefs such as "I can't do anything right," instead of believing the thought say: "I just had a thought that I can't do anything right". That creates some space between the thought and you so that you don't have be activated by the thought. You just notice that thinking is happening, and you don't pay attention to the content of the thought. Just say, "there's that thought again". Don't get activated by the thought.

Practice: Dis-identifying from the fixed self

When you give attention to the present moment, and notice your sense perceptions (what you see, what you hear, what you feel, what you taste) you can't distinguish a boundary between the person experiencing the sensations and the sensations themselves. There's just awareness of the sensations. There is no "person" seeing, listening, tasting, etc. There is just seeing, listening, tasting being experienced.

So ultimately that's all there is. There is awareness but there's no fixed "self" that you can perceive seeing the images, listening to the sounds, etc. Listen to the sounds in the room right now and notice if you can find the boundary between the sounds and the person or "self" listening to the sounds. There's just sound. Where is the self? There is just awareness of the sound.

Now focus on something you can see right now. If there is a clock in the room or a picture, or a chair, focus on the seeing then ask yourself, 'who is seeing?'.

Experience the moment

Be in the moment and leave no trace. Don't try to accumulate knowledge or gain anything from mindfulness. That's just more ego becoming attached to something.

Just experience the moment and don't strive to attain anything or become anyone.

Reflection:

What would your life look like if you were living in a state of inner peace?

Whatever you create externally is a direct reflection of your inner state.

Now is the most important moment of your life.

Celebrating the Now

The following are simple practices you can establish daily to keep you in the now. These practices are intended to bring awareness to the now by replacing phrases that are time-based (Fridays, 'special' days like New Years) with phrases that focus on the now.

TGIN

Instead of the traditional TGIF (thank God it's Friday), you can use TGIN (Thank God it's Now). TGIN reminds you to be grateful for the present moment, the most important moment, because you are alive right now!

Happy New Day!

Instead of only celebrating certain days of the year, make every day a celebration! Wish everyone around you a happy new day. When you wake up, you can tell others happy new day instead of the traditional good morning. It can help you remember that every day is special because you are living it!

How can you make the most difference in the world?

Be present with whoever is right in front of you. Give people your full attention at all times and see what transpires. The quality of your interactions will increase, you will experience a deep sense of fulfillment. You do not need to travel across the world to make a difference. You can make a difference every day, every moment, right where you are.

"May you live every day of your life."
Jonathan Swift